Dr. Seuss Workbook

PHONICS

LEVEL 1

Let's Learn to Read!

Welcome to Dr. Seuss Workbooks, where kids learn and practice important skills they'll use in the classroom and beyond!

This book teaches reading through **phonics**, which helps children match written letters and spoken sounds.

Your child will learn to read words by putting together sounds, either from single letters or word chunks.

Along the way, they will also learn many **sight words.**

Sight words are words you learn to recognize by sight. Some of these are important words that might not follow the rules of spelling and may not be easy to recognize just by putting together letter sounds.

On some pages, you'll see this icon. It indicates a place where your child is encouraged to read out loud. Help them get comfortable matching letters with sounds. That's phonics!

See it, say it!

We hope your child has tons of fun with these activities as they play, laugh…and read!

–Your friends at Dr. Seuss

Ready, Set, Alphabet!

Write the letters of the alphabet in order. Put one in each space. The first one has been done for you.

As you write each letter, say the sound that it makes.

Meet Short A

The word **hat** has a **short a** sound in the middle.

Write the letter **a** to finish each word, then say the word aloud.

h__m   s__d   f__n

j__m   b__t   m__d

See it, say it!

What sound does **short a** make? Say it three times.

Circle four things that have a **short a** sound.

Draw something that has the **short a** sound.

Words with _at

The word **cat** ends with **at**.

Write **at** to finish each word.

h_____   r_____   s_____

spl_____   c_____   b_____

Draw a path from each picture to the matching word that ends in **at**.

hop

hit

run

sun

cat

pig

bug

sit

hat

sip

ten

fit

rat

pig

cup

dog

Words with _an

The word **pan** ends with **an**.

Write **an** to finish each word.

p____   f____   m_____

t____   c_____   v____

Find a path from **START** to **END**. You can only go through words that end in **an**.

START

vet — can — van — pot

tip — jug

jug — hip — tub — cup

ran — sip — bat — hat

man

knot

tan — log

mug — gum

jar — man

rug — cat — fan — ban

bug — rat — ran — sun

bad — pan

car — van

END

11

Words with _ap

The word **map** ends with **ap**.

Write **ap** to finish each word.

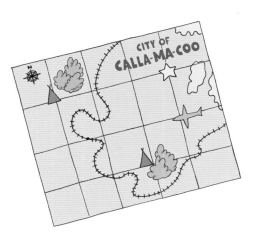

m____   c____   y____

n____   z____   t____

Circle all the words that end in **ap**.

gap

rap

zap

lap

pup

hot

fit

big

sap

Circle the words that end in **ap** in this puzzle.
They go up, down, and across. Use the words in
the word box to help you.

| cap | sap | tap | nap |

T C A P P P

A F E G A

P W O R S

N A P S Z

Sight Words

Color each of these new sight words.

she he

the is

Write each word and say it aloud.

See it,
say it!

_____   _____

_____   _____

Draw a line between each matching word.

a   one

am   do

do   by

one   a

by   am

Cross out the ones that are not real words.

it

was

a   brg   has

if

is

tfz

at

inx

ppp

Word Fun

Follow each trail and write the word the letters make in the space at the end.

_____ _____ _____

Unscramble the letters and write the word next to each picture.

n a f

t b a

t c a

p a c

A Review for You!

Trace each line. Write the words the letters make.

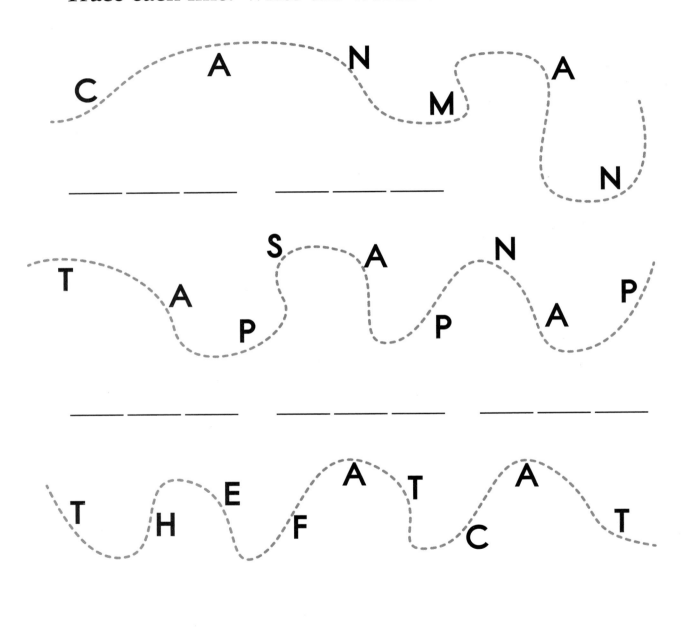

____ ____

____ ____ ____

____ ____ ____

See it, say it!

Say each word aloud.

Circle all the words that end with an.

The man sat.

Pat can tap a pan.

The fan is red.

Sam has a van.

The cat ran.

Dan had a jar.

Read each sentence above.
You can do it!

19

Meet Short E

The word **red** has a **short e** sound in the middle.

Write the letter **e** to finish each word, then say the word aloud.

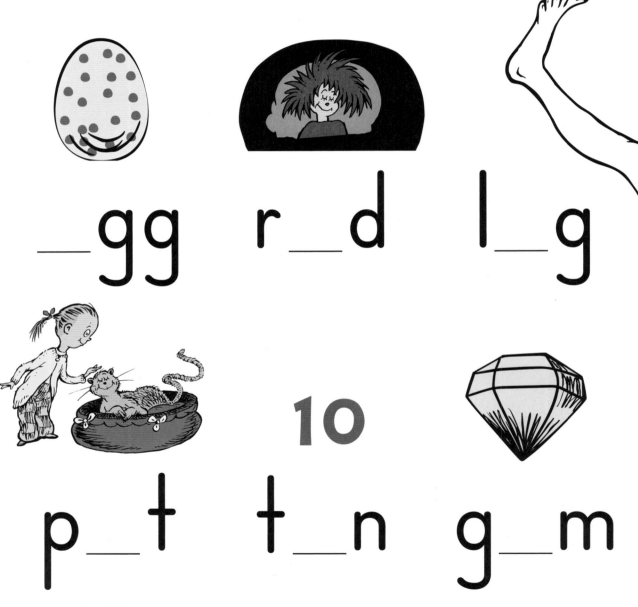

_gg   r_d   l_g

p_t   t_n   g_m

See it, say it!

What sound does **short e** make? Say it three times.

Circle four things that have a **short e** sound.

Draw something that has the **short e** sound.

Words with _et

The word **set** ends with **et**.

Write **et** to finish each word.

w___ p___ n___

j___ m___ v___

Draw a path from each picture to the matching word that ends in **et**.

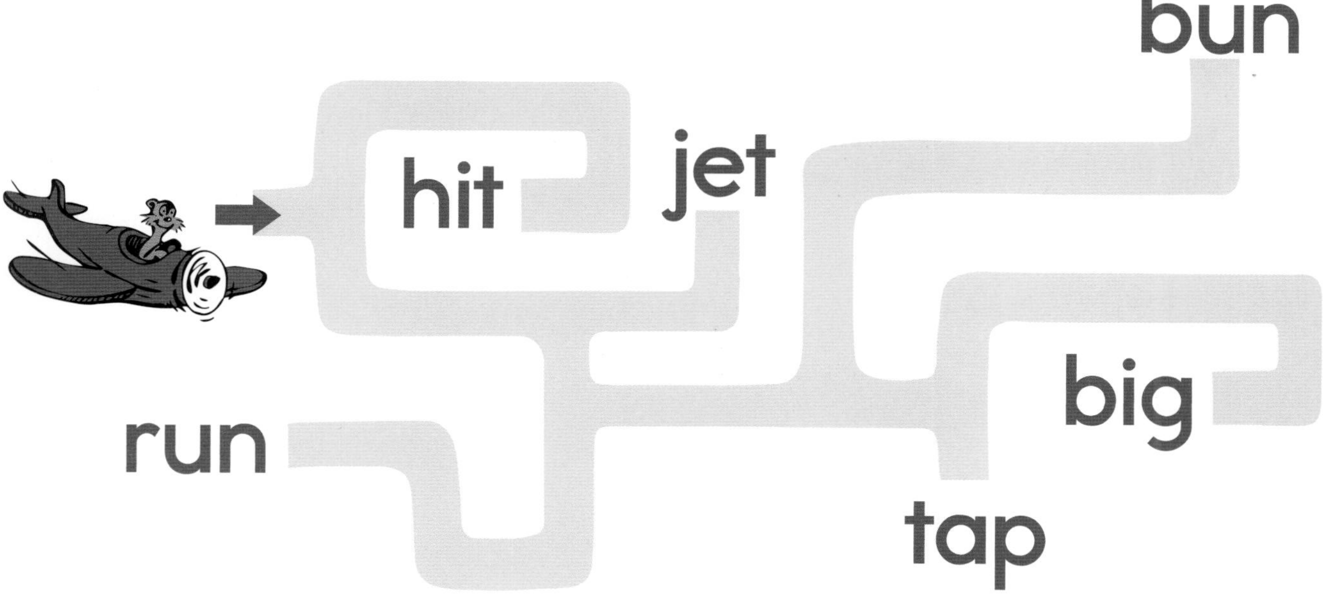

bun

hit jet

run

big

tap

mug

tip

dog

bug

met

sip

net

pin

can dug

Words with _en

The word **ten** ends with **en**.

Write **en** to finish each word.

op_____

t_____

m_____

p_____

z_____

h_____

Find a path from **START** to **END**. You can only go through words that end in **en**.

START

END

Words with _ed

The word **fed** ends with **ed**.

Write **ed** to finish each word.

sl_____

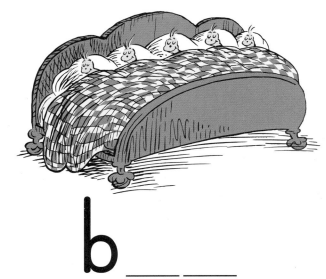

b_____

r_____

f_____

Circle all the words that end in **ed**.

top

sped

hip

red

wed

fed

led

bed

rat

Circle the words that end in **ed** in this puzzle.
They go up, down, and across. Use the words in
the word box to help you.

led	wed	fed	red

L H F E D

E D R E D

D E O R Z

J W P L U

Sight Words

Color each of these new sight words.

out for
and if

Write each word and say it aloud.

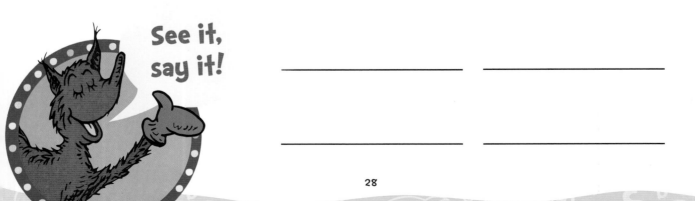

See it,
say it!

_____   _____

_____   _____

Draw a line between each matching word.

been   with

see   into

with   see

into   come

come   been

Cross out the ones that are not real words.

he   mfn

tji   and   she

if   I

my   ydt

one   irg

Word Fun

Trace each line and write the word the letters make in the space at the end.

Unscramble the letters and write the word next to each picture.

_____

h n e

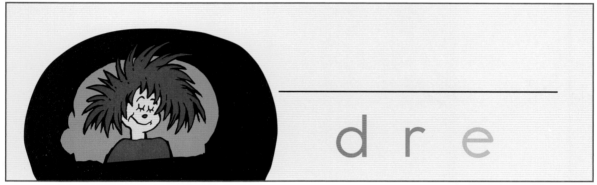

_____

d r e

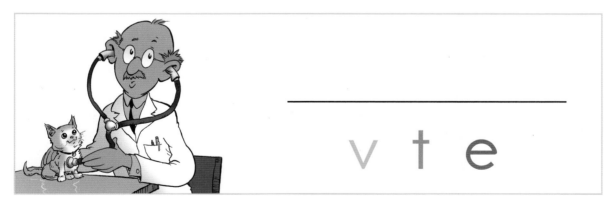

_____

v t e

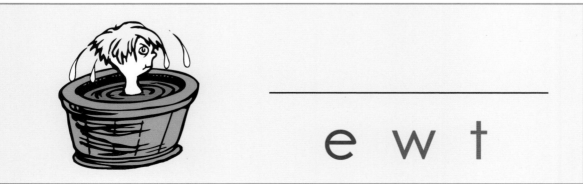

_____

e w t

A New Review!

Trace each line. Write the words the letters make.

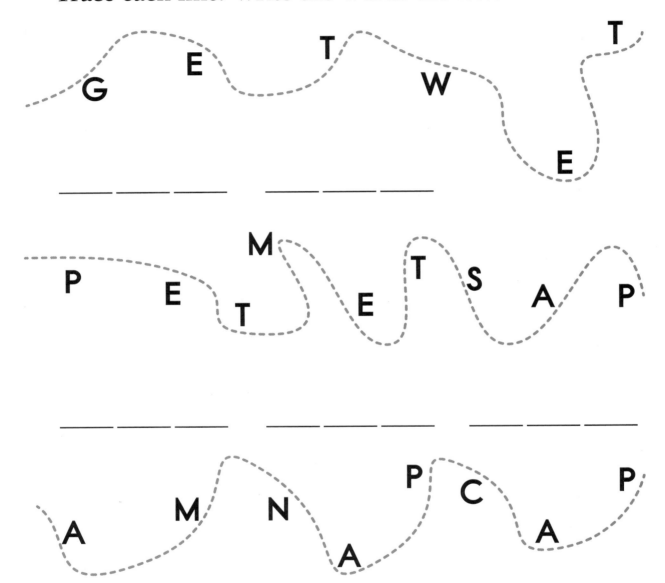

G   E   T   W   T   E

___ ___ ___   ___ ___ ___

P   E   M   T   E   T   S   A   P

___ ___ ___   ___ ___ ___   ___ ___ ___

A   M   N   P   A   C   A   P

___ ___ ___   ___ ___ ___   ___ ___ ___

See it, say it!   Say each word aloud.

Circle all the words that end with **et** or **ap**.

The vet saw a hen.

The man had a nap.

If I get a pan, I am fed.

She has a map.

Dan has a pet.

The cap was wet.

See it, say it!

Read each sentence above.
You can do it!

Look What S Can Do

Add an **s** to a word to make one into many.

Write the letter **s** at the end of each word, then say the word aloud.

hen___

cat___

can___

egg___

Circle four things that have an s sound at the end.

Draw something that starts with s. Then draw something that ends with s.

More With S, Not Less

Follow the trail from **START** to **END**. Look at each picture you pass and circle the correct matching word. The first one has been done to show you how.

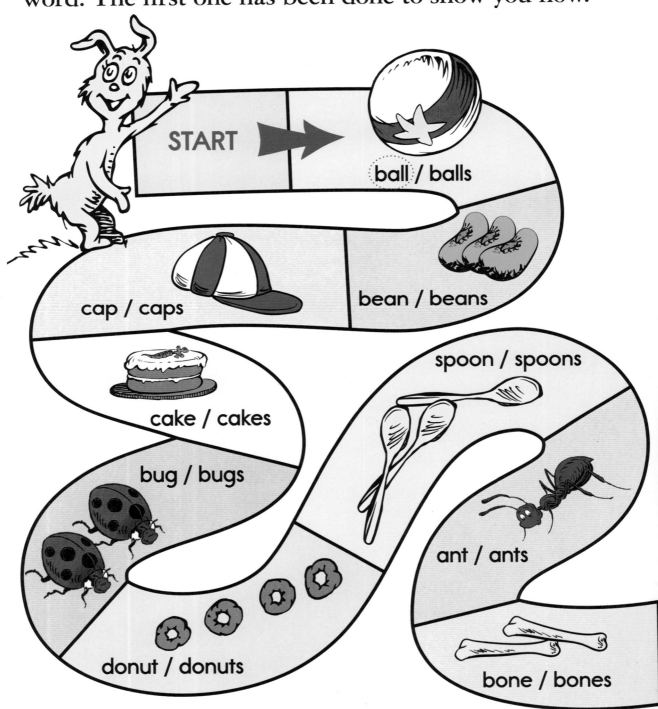

START

ball / balls

cap / caps

bean / beans

cake / cakes

spoon / spoons

bug / bugs

ant / ants

donut / donuts

bone / bones

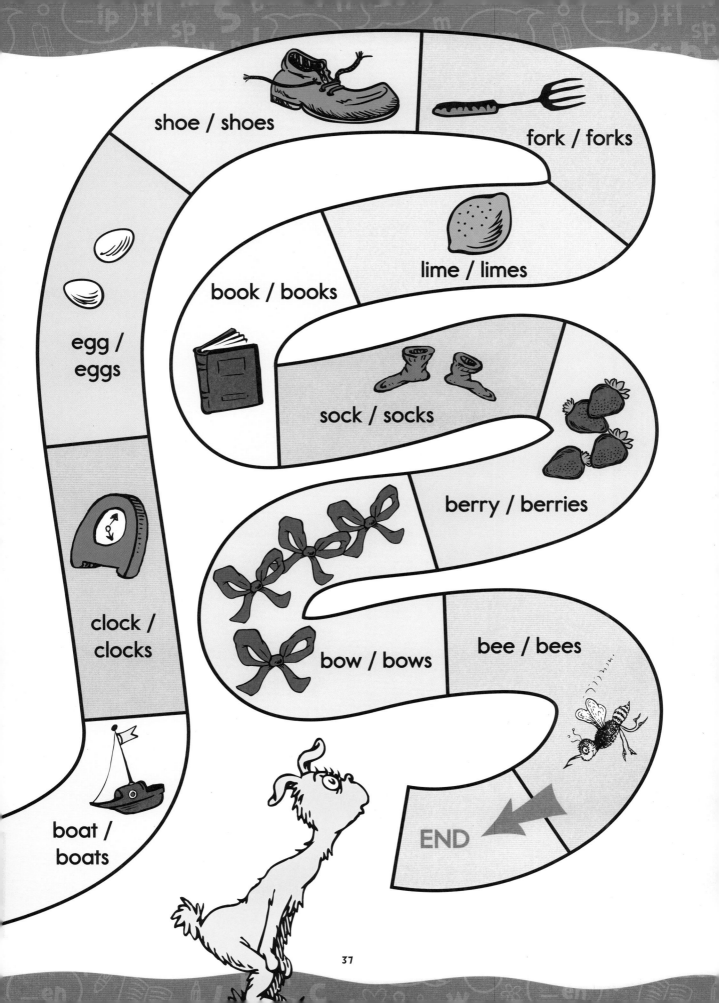

shoe / shoes

fork / forks

lime / limes

book / books

egg / eggs

sock / socks

berry / berries

clock / clocks

bow / bows

bee / bees

boat / boats

END

A Wild Ride

Draw a path from **START** to **END**. You can only pass through real words.

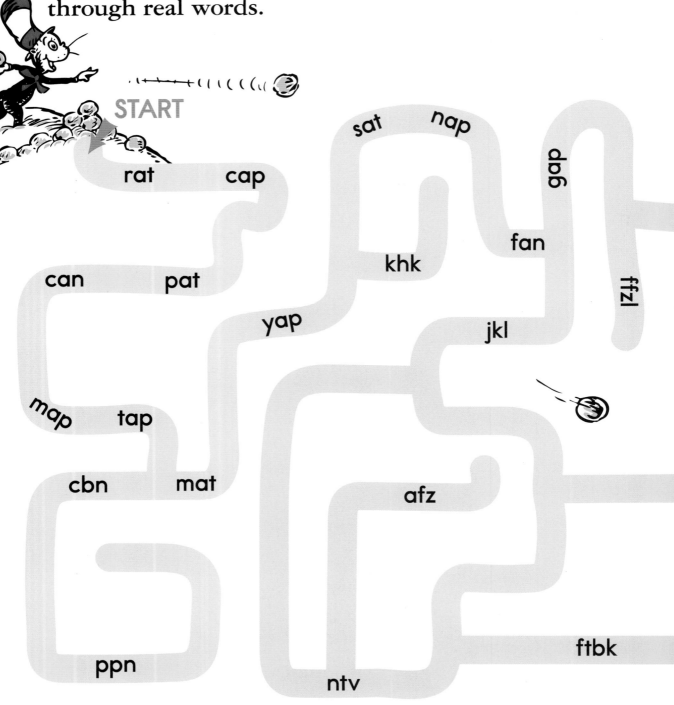

START

rat · cap

sat · nap

gap

fan

can · pat

khk

ffzl

yap

jkl

map · tap

cbn · mat

afz

ppn

ntv

ftbk

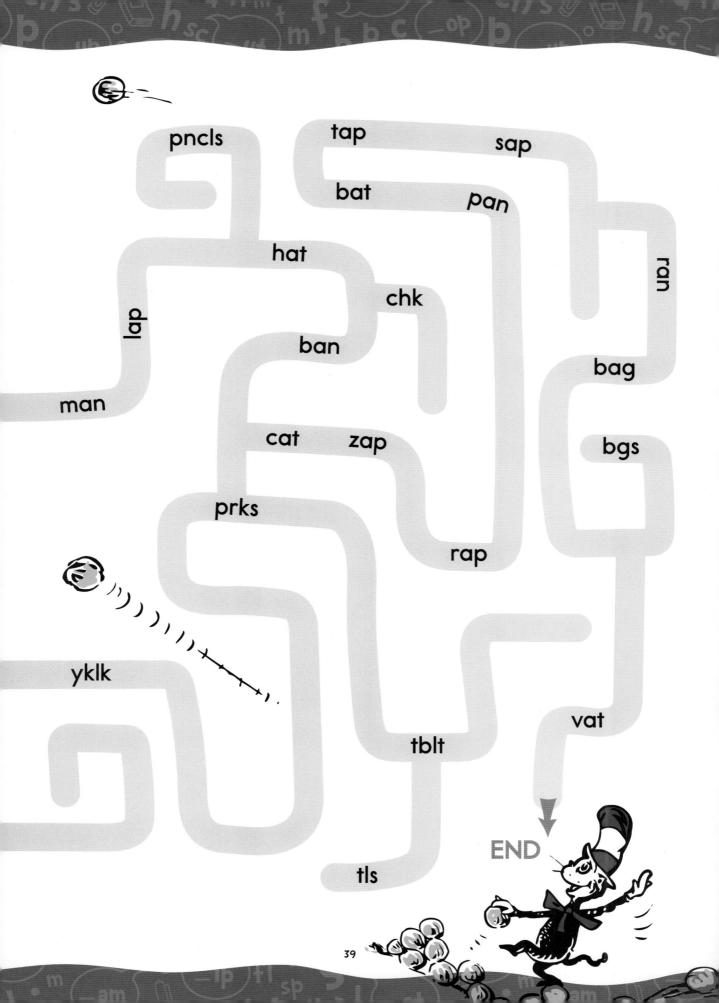

pncls

tap

sap

bat

pan

hat

ran

chk

ban

lap

bag

man

cat

zap

bgs

prks

rap

yklk

vat

tblt

END

tls

Meet Short I

The word **pin** has a **short** i sound in the middle.

Write the letter i to finish each word, then say the word aloud.

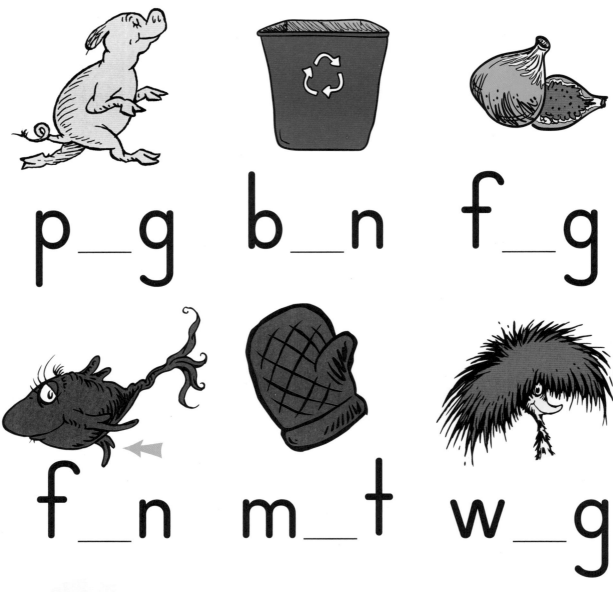

p_g   b__n   f__g

f__n   m__t   w__g

See it, say it!

What sound does **short** i make? Say it three times.

Circle four things that have a **short i** sound.

Draw something that has the **short i** sound.

Words with _in

The word **win** ends with **in**.

Write **in** to finish each word.

b____ gr_____ f_____

t____ tw____ p____

Draw a path from each picture to the matching word
that ends in **in**.

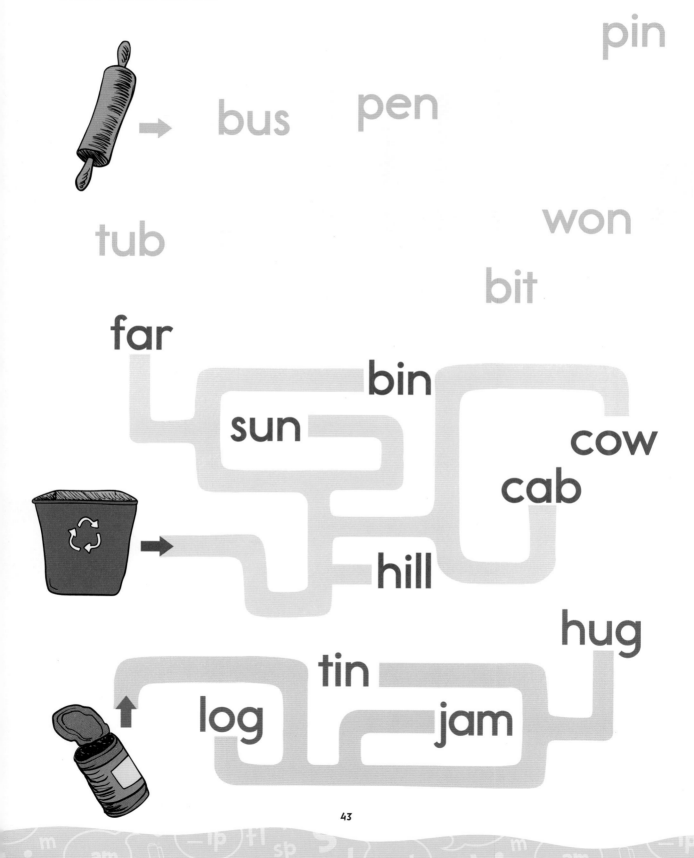

pin

bus   pen

won

tub

bit

far

bin

sun

cow

cab

hill

hug

tin

log   jam

Words with _it

The word **pit** ends with it.

Write **it** to finish each word.

p___   h___   m___

b___   kn___   s___

44

Find a path from **START** to **END**. You can only go through words that end in **it**.

START

pit

pin

win

hit

nap

hat

zap   pat   sap   fit   bun

vet   sip

sit   bit

lap

tin

zit

pot

kit   win

lap   wig   tin

wit   cat   fig

sit   fat   get

win   nit

sun   nit

sat   bit

lit

END

Words with _ip

The word **rip** ends with **ip**.

Write **ip** to finish each word.

s____

t____

sn____

n____

Circle all the words that end in **ip**.

sip

mop

dip

hip

cap

tip

nip

ten

bun

Circle the words that end in **ip** in this puzzle. They go up, down, and across. Use the words in the word box to help you.

| zip | rip | hip | lip |

J	R	I	P	I
I	Z	Y	P	H
D	I	O	I	I
J	P	N	L	P

Sight Words

Color each of these new sight words.

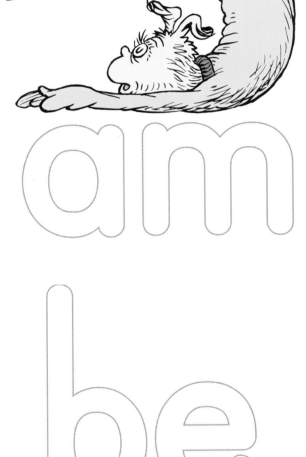

by am

as be

Write each word and say it aloud.

See it, say it!

_____   _____

_____   _____

Draw a line between each matching word.

all   she

each   day

she   but

but   each

day   all

Cross out the ones that are not real words.

nohp   px

         but   by

weu   if   be

         am   sta

   go   all

49

Word Fun

Trace each line and write the word the letters make in the space at the end.

Unscramble the letters and write the word next to each picture.

p n i

i s t

i f n

s p i

Show What You Know

Trace each line. Write the words the letters make.

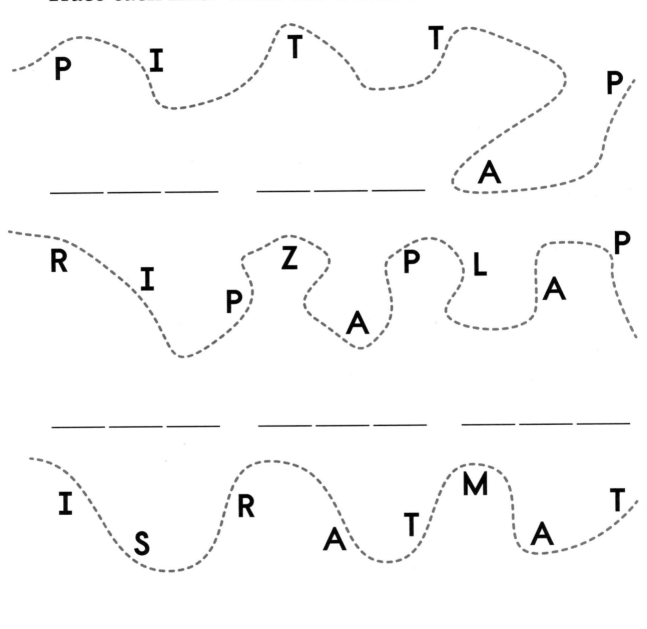

_____ _____

_____ _____ _____

_____ _____ _____

See it, say it!

Say each word aloud.

Circle all the words that end with **at** or **ip**.

The cat has a hat.

I can go zip, zip, zip.

I see a fat rat.

He will sip.

Pat sat on the mat.

She will dip that chip.

See it, say it!

Read each sentence above. You can do it!

Meet Short O

The word **log** has a **short o** sound in the middle.

Write the letter **o** to finish each word, then say the word aloud.

h__t　　st__p　　t__p

f__x　　b__x　　m__p

What sound does **short o** make? Say it three times.

Circle four things that have a **short o** sound.

Draw something that has the **short o** sound.

Words with _op

The word **hop** ends with **op**.

Write **op** to finish each word.

h____

p____

t____

m____

Draw a path from each picture to the matching word that ends in **op**.

bat

get

tin

mop

nap

pit

vet

sip

cut

ten

hop

bib

win

leg

den

top

Words with _ot

The word **lot** ends with **ot**.

Write **ot** to finish each word.

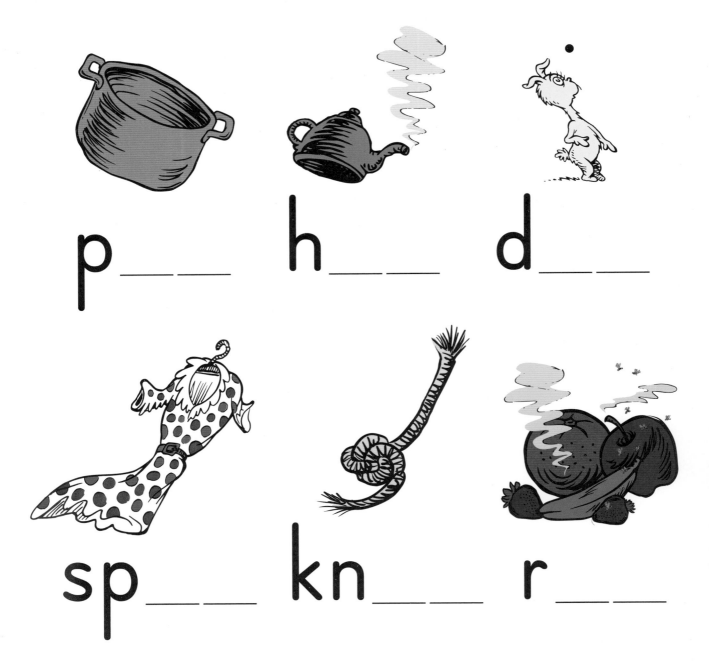

p____   h____   d____

sp____   kn____   r____

Find a path from **START** to **END**. You can only go through words that end in **ot**.

START

not

kin

pan

pot

pet

rot

yet

pen

cot

ran

jot

set

got

lit

lot

cat

pat

bat

log

jig

tot

bog

big

pig

sip

lip

cot

fin

lot

fig

hot

wig

dog

dot

spot

END

Words with _ox and _ob

The word **fox** ends with **ox**.

Write **ox** to finish each word.

f____

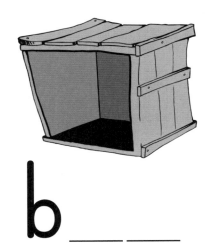

b____

The word **job** ends with **ob**.

Write **ob** to finish each word.

s____

bl____

Circle all the words that end in **ox** or **ob**.

cob

nob

box

sob

rip

pin

can

lob

lox

Circle the words that end in **ox** and **ob** in this puzzle. They go up, down, and across. Use the words in the word box to help you.

nob	rob	fox	box

M A B E D

R F O X B

O B O X O

B E O Z N

Sight Words

Color each of these new sight words.

do one

a that

Write each word and say it aloud.

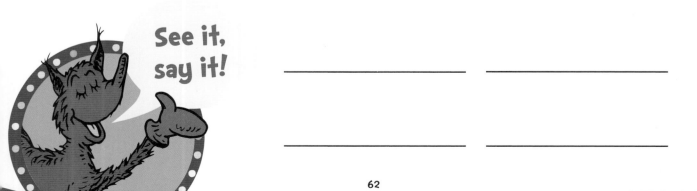

**See it,
say it!**

_____ _____

_____ _____

Draw a line between each matching word.

that   you

each   is

you   but

but   each

is   that

Cross out the ones that are not real words.

this   my

you   itw   rra

zsg   is

do   ppo

be

and

Word Fun

Trace each line and write the word the letters make in the space at the end.

P
C
R
O
O
O
P T
B

_____ _____ _____

Unscramble the letters and write the word next to each picture.

o x b

t p o

x o f

m p o

What's New? A Review!

Trace each line. Write the words the letters make.

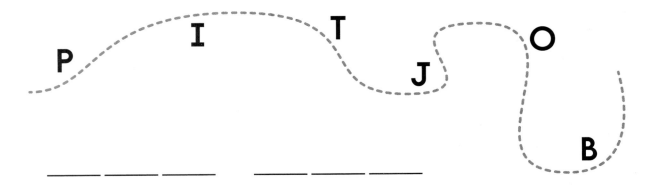

___ ___ ___ ___ ___ ___

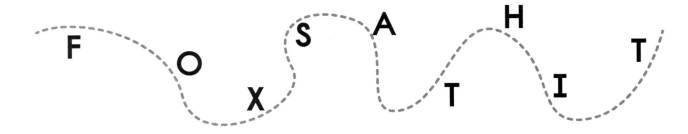

___ ___ ___ ___ ___ ___ ___

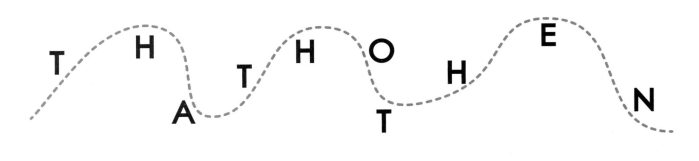

___ ___ ___ ___ ___ ___ ___

See it, say it!

Say each word aloud.

Circle all the words that end with **ox** or **it**.

That is my box.

Hop by that fox.

Hit this top and go.

He bit the lox.

She fit in the pit.

The ox can sit.

See it, say it!

Read each sentence above.
You can do it!

67

Meet Short U

The word **bun** has a **short u** sound in the middle.

Write the letter **u** to finish each word, then say the word aloud.

c_p

p_p

s_n

b_g

j_g

r_n

See it, say it!

What sound does **short u** make? Say it three times.

Circle four things that have a **short u** sound.

Draw something that has the **short u** sound.

Words with _un

The word **fun** ends with **un**.

Write **un** to finish each word.

r _____

s _____

sp _____

b _____

Draw a path from each picture to the matching word that ends in **un**.

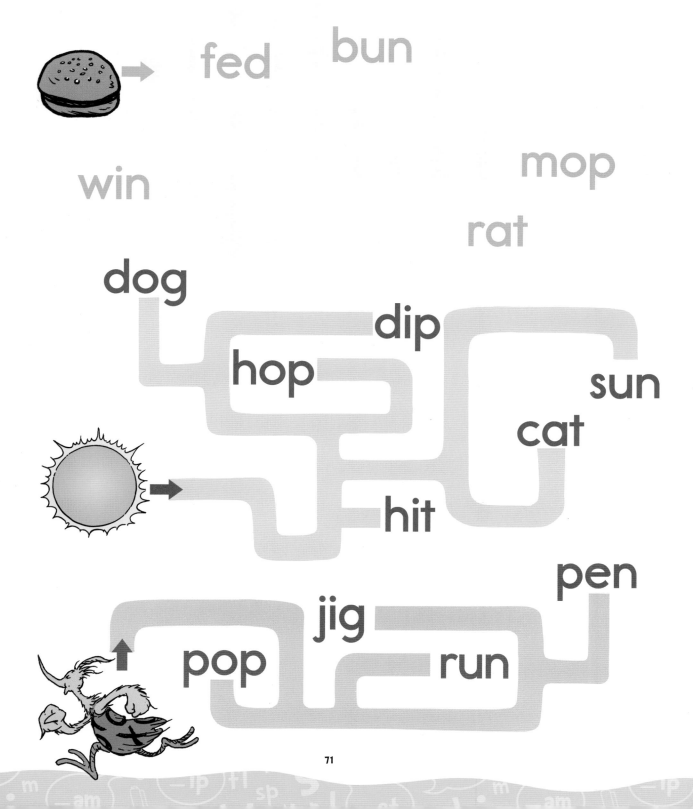

sit

fed   bun

win   mop

        rat

dog

        dip

    hop   sun

                    cat

        hit

                    pen

            jig

    pop   run

Words with _ug

The word **pug** ends with **ug**.

Write **ug** to finish each word.

b____

h____

j____

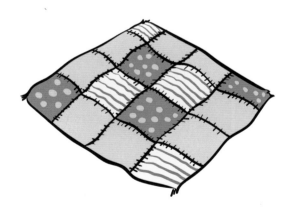

r____

Find a path from **START** to **END**. You can only go through words that end in **ug**.

START

END

Words with _up and _ub

The word **sup** ends with **up**.

Write **up** to finish each word.

c_____

p_____

The word **rub** ends with **ub**.

Write **ub** to finish each word.

s_____

t_____

Circle all the words that end in **up** or **ub**.

cub   pup

top   sub

pan   rub

tub

cup   ran

Circle the words that end in **up** and **ub** in this puzzle. They go up, down, and across. Use the words in the word box to help you.

pup	cup	tub	rub

M   R   U   B   P

P   F   A   N   U

U   T   U   B   P

C   B   E   D   U

Sight Words

Color each of these new sight words.

up we

in of

Write each word and say it aloud.

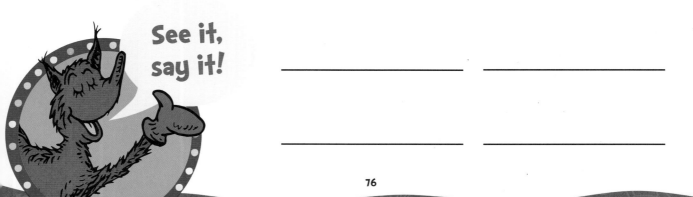

See it, say it!

_____ _____

_____ _____

Draw a line between each matching word.

this	that
when	this
then	made
that	then
made	when

Cross out the ones that are not real words.

sizz

of

exu

she

but

up

jba

eer

in

when

we

Word Fun

Follow each trail and write the word the letters make in the space at the end.

_____ _____

Unscramble the letters and write the word next to each picture.

c b u

b g u

n u s

p p u

Test Your Skills

Trace each line. Write the words the letters make.

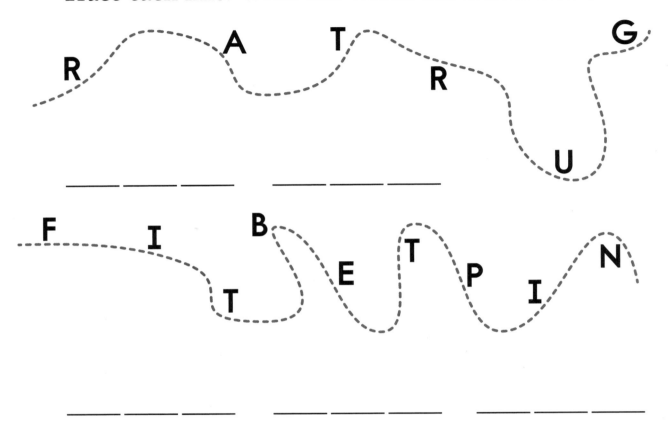

R A T T R R G U

___ ___ ___ ___ ___ ___

F I T B E T P I N

___ ___ ___ ___ ___ ___ ___ ___ ___

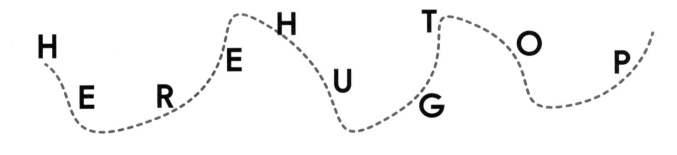

H E R E H U G T O P

___ ___ ___ ___ ___ ___

Say each word aloud.

Circle all the words that end with up or ed.

We can hop on the bed.

She sips the cup.

Where is my pup?

That man has a red hat.

I ran up the hill.

Ted is sad.

See it, say it!

Read each sentence above.
You can do it!

Meet the Vowel Y

The word **try** has a **vowel** y sound at the end.

Write the letter y to finish each word, then say the word aloud.

fl__

sk__

sl__

cr__

See it, say it!

What sound can the letter y make when it is a vowel? Say it three times.

Circle all the words that end in **vowel y**.

try

fly

guy

sky

sly

my

top

cub

dry

cry

by

pin

bed

Draw something that ends with **vowel y**.

Oh My! It's Y!

Draw a path from **START** to **END**. You can only pass through a word if it ends with **vowel y**.

START

guy

fly   cry

why

dry   sly   bun   kit

by   buy

ten

try   sky

bin   my   ten

pan

tin   pen

ju

run

spy

sly

ply

won   car

fin

wry

van

lit

shy

pry

rat

cry

fry

my

sly

why

ran

END

cat

Sight Words

Color each of these new sight words.

at are

there

Write each word and say it aloud.

See it, say it!

_____ _____

_____

Draw a line between each matching word.

play   at

at   down

are   play

here   are

down   here

Cross out the ones that are not real words.

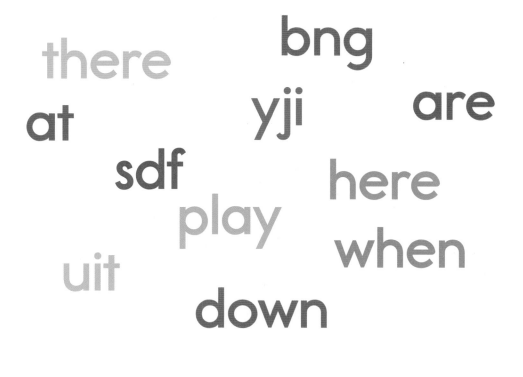

there   bng   are

at   yji

sdf   here

play   when

uit   down

Word Fun

Trace each line and write the word the letters make in the space at the end.

_____   _____   _____

Unscramble the letters and write the word next to each picture.

_____

e s e

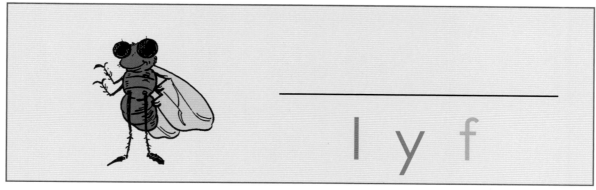

_____

l y f

_____

y l p a

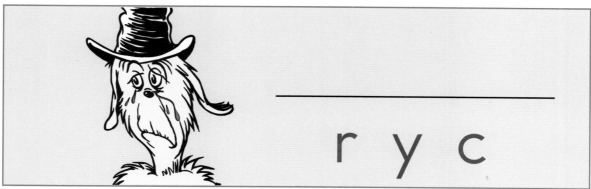

_____

r y c

Hop to It!

Find a path from **START** to **END**. You can only pass through real words.

START

can   ibn

hat

zte   mnct   egg

den

flsy

fat

nmn   gem

yap   prdly

brc

lion   gft   bell

dot   pop

nit

pin   jmbre

snip

this

hit   hen   hot

sun

mop   fox   drum

hill

bug

END

ANSWERS

Pages 4–5

Page 7

Page 9
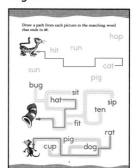

Page 11

Page 13

Page 15
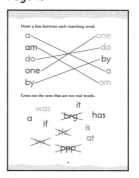

Pages 16–17
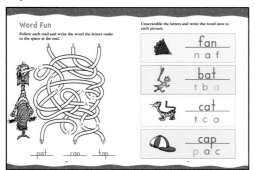

Pages 18–19

Page 21

Page 23

Page 25

Page 27
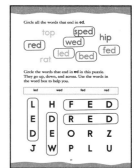

Page 29

Pages 30–31

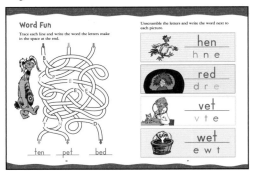

Pages 32–33

Page 35

Pages 36–37

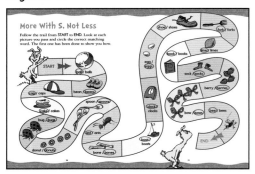

Pages 38–39

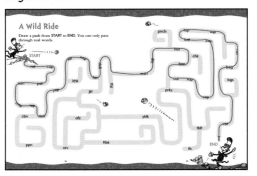

Page 41

Page 43

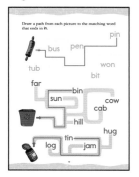

Page 45

Page 47

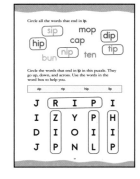

Draw a line between each matching word.

all — she
each — day
she — but
but — each
day — all

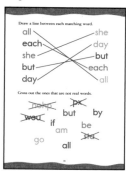

Cross out the ones that are not real words.

~~tokp~~ ~~px~~ by
~~wou~~ if be
am ~~sto~~
go all

Word Fun

Trace each line and write the word the letters make in the space at the end.

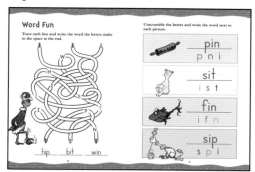

hip bit win

Unscramble the letters and write the word next to each picture.

pin
p n i

sit
i s t

fin
i f n

sip
s p i

Show What You Know

Trace each line. Write the words the letters make.

pit tap

rip zap lap

is rat mat

See it, say it! Say each word aloud.

Circle all the words that end with **at** or **ip**.

The (cat) has a (hat)
I can go (zip) (zip) (zip)
I see a (fat) (rat)
He will (sip)
(Pat) (sat) on the (mat)
She will (dip) (that) (chip)

See it, say it! Read each sentence above. You can do it!

Circle four things that have a **short a** sound.

Draw something that has the **short** o sound.

Draw a path from each picture to the matching word that ends in **op**.

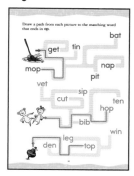

bat
get tin
mop nap
vet pit
sip
cut ten
bib hop
win
den leg top

Find a path from **START** to **END**. You can only go through words that end in **ot**.

START
END

Circle all the words that end in **ox** or **ob**.

(cob) (nob)
rip (sob) (box)
(lox) can (lob) pin

Circle the words that end in **ox** and **ob** in this puzzle. They go up, down, and across. Use the words in the word box to help you.

| nob | rob | fox | box |

M A B E D
R (F O X) B
O (B O X) O N
B E O Z N

Draw a line between each matching word.

that — you
each — is
you — but
but — each
is — that

Cross out the ones that are not real words.

this my
you ~~tht~~ ~~tro~~
~~zsg~~ is
be do ~~ppo~~
and

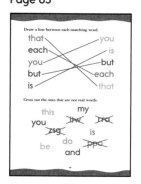

Pages 64–65

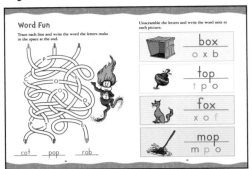

Word Fun

Trace each line and write the word the letters make in the space at the end.

Unscramble the letters and write the word next to each picture.

box
o x b

top
t p o

fox
x o f

mop
m p o

cot   pop   rob

Pages 66–67

What's New? A Review!

Trace each line. Write the words the letters make.

pit job

fox sat hit

that hot hen

Say each word aloud.

Circle all the words that end with ox or it.

That is my (box.)

Hop by that (fox.)

(Hit) this top and go.

He bit the (lox.)

She (fit) in the (pit.)

The (ox) can (sit.)

Read each sentence above. You can do it!

Page 69

Circle four things that have a short u sound.

Draw something that has the short u sound.

Page 71

Draw a path from each picture to the matching word that ends in un.

sit

fed   bun

mop

win   rat

dog   dip

hop   sun

hit   cat

pen

pop jig run

Page 73

Find a path from START to END. You can only go through words that end in ug.

START

END

Page 75

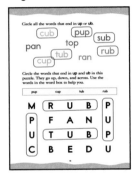

Circle all the words that end in up or ub.

(cub) (pup) (sub)

pan   top   (rub)

(cup) (tub) ran

Circle the words that end in up and ub in this puzzle. They go up, down, and across. Use the words in the word box to help you.

| pup | cup | tub | rub |

M	R	U	B	P
P	F	A	N	U
P	U	T	U	B	P
U	C	B	E	D	U

Page 77

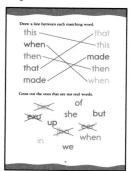

Pages 78–79

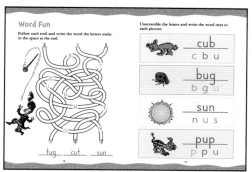

Pages 80–81

Page 83

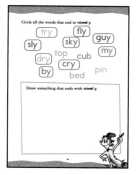

Pages 84–85

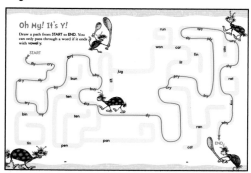

Page 87

Pages 88–89

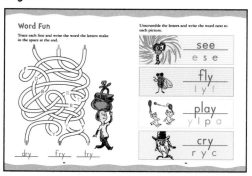

Page 90

Your brand-new skills
are just what you need.

HOORAY FOR

_____

NAME

who is learning to read!

Phonics Level 1

CERTIFICATE OF ACHIEVEMENT